EXPLORING EARTH'S · BIOMES ·

WETLAND

APRIL PULLEY SAYRE

TF CB

TWENTY-FIRST CENTURY BOOKS

A Division of Henry Holt and Company
• New York •

*For Maxine Watts, in thanks for her swamp
stories and our bayou adventures.*

ACKNOWLEDGMENTS
Our thanks to Dr. John Waldman of the Hudson River Foundation, who reviewed portions of this manuscript.

Twenty-First Century Books
A Division of Henry Holt and Company, Inc.
115 West 18th Street
New York, NY 10011

Henry Holt ® and colophon are trademarks of
Henry Holt and Company, Inc.
Publishers since 1866

Library of Congress Cataloging-in-Publication Data
Sayre, April Pulley.
Wetland / April Pulley Sayre.—1st ed.
p. cm.—(Exploring earth's biomes)
Includes index.
Summary: Discusses the wetland biome and how
it is affected by the environment and people.
1. Wetland ecology—Juvenile literature. 2. Wetlands—Juvenile literature.
3. Wetland ecology—North America—Juvenile literature. 4. Wetlands—North
America—Juvenile literature. [1. Wetlands. 2. Wetland ecology. 3. Ecology.] I. Title.
II. Series: Sayre, April Pulley. Exploring earth's biomes.
QH541.5.M3S27 1996   574.5'26325—dc20
95-36227   CIP
                                                                AC

ISBN 0-8050-4086-2
First Edition—1996

Cover design by Betty Lew
Interior design by Kelly Soong

Printed in the United States of America
All first editions are printed on acid-free paper ∞.
10 9 8 7 6 5 4 3 2 1

Photo credits appear on page 78.

CONTENTS

INTRODUCTION TO AQUATIC BIOMES

The water that makes up more than two-thirds of your body weight, that flows in your blood, that bathes your cells, and that you cry as tears, may once have flowed in a river. It may have floated as a cloud, fallen as a snowflake, bobbed in ocean waves, or been drunk by a dinosaur from an ancient lake. All this is possible because the water that's presently on earth has always been here—except for ice brought by comets hitting the earth's atmosphere. And all the water on earth is connected in a global cycle. This cycle is called the water cycle, or the hydrologic cycle.

Every day, all over the earth, water exists in and moves through this cycle. Ninety-seven percent of the earth's water is in the oceans. Two percent is in frozen glaciers and ice caps at the Poles. The remaining 1 percent is divided among the world's lakes, rivers, groundwater, soil moisture, and water vapor in the air. All this comes to a grand total of 326 million cubic miles (1,359 million cubic kilometers) of water. Every day, this water is exchanged among the oceans, streams, clouds, glaciers, lakes, wetlands, and even dew-covered leaves. Even now, it is being exhaled from your body, as moisture in your breath.

As the water cycles, at times it changes phase from solid to liquid to gas. The heat of the sun warms water on the land's surface, in lakes, in streams, in the ocean, even on the leaves of plants—and causes this water to evaporate, to turn into a gas. This gas rises into the air, cools, and condenses, eventually forming clouds and falling back to earth as liquid rain or solid snow or hail. This precipitation makes its way into streams, rivers, lakes, oceans, glaciers, and ice caps, and underground. And so the cycle continues. But it's not quite so simple. Each portion of the cycle is connected to others. For example, river water runs into oceans, stream water runs into lakes, and water from underground bubbles out of springs and into rivers. Water is constantly being exchanged among all the many places it resides on planet earth.

Almost anywhere water exists as a liquid, it is colonized by organisms—bacteria, amoebas, fungi, animals, or plants. Some watery habitats have particular physical conditions and particular kinds of plants and animals inhabiting them. These are aquatic biomes: ocean, river, lake, and coral reef. Where these aquatic biomes mingle with terrestrial, or land, biomes, they may form special, semiaquatic, fringe communities. Wetland and seashore are two of these communities that are unique enough and widespread enough to qualify as major biomes.

All aquatic and semiaquatic biomes—ocean, river, lake, coral reef, seashore, and wetland—are influenced by regional climate and the lands nearby. These biomes are also linked to one another, by ever-moving water molecules and the global water cycle through which they flow.

❅ 1 ❅
THE WETLAND BIOME

Soggy, boggy, wet, and wonderful, wetlands are places where strange things happen. In Michigan bogs, plants use sticky lures and water-filled pits to capture insects. In African marshes, antelope avoid predators by hiding underwater. In the Amazon's flooded forests, fish swim among tree branches, picking fruit and dropping seeds. And in South Carolina swamps, plants perch on trees, nurtured by no more than water and minerals in the air.

Simply put, wetlands are just what their name says: wet land. Their soils are soggy and flooded. But they may not stay that way all the time. Most wetlands go through daily, monthly, or seasonal wet/dry cycles. High tide floods a coastal marsh, but at low tide it may bake dry in the sun. Wet meadows can be sodden after spring rains but dry enough for a farmer to plow them in summer. Bogs, moist and squishy in spring, can become so dry in the summer that a bolt of lightning sets them aflame.

Like rain forest and coral reef, wetland is a biome—an area that has a certain kind of community of animals and plants. Yet, unlike desert, tundra, and other terrestrial biomes, wetland does not have a characteristic climate. Wetlands vary widely in composition and are strongly influenced by the land biomes and aquatic biomes that surround them. Wetlands occur on the fringes of other aquatic

Wetlands provide important habitats
for ducks and other migratory birds.

biomes: on lake margins, river edges, and ocean shores. Or, they may exist on their own, forming pockets in the prairie, breaks in the forest, or soggy, mountaintop habitats. Wherever they exist, wetlands tend to have special kinds of soils, which develop under waterlogged conditions, and plants that have adapted to those soils.

Wetlands vary tremendously, from the cold, damp bogs of Finland to the sweltering swamp forests of Zaire; from the cool, windswept salt marshes of Canada's Hudson Bay to the tangled coastal mangroves of Bangladesh. Wetlands may occur inland or close to the coast, where they're affected by ocean tides. They may contain salt water or fresh water, or a mixture of the two. Their plants may vary in height and growth pattern. And their animals can be diverse. Wetlands are home to manatees, wood storks, snail kites, Pine Barrens tree frogs, crocodiles, snakes, turtles, and more. This book focuses on North America, which contains many wetland types and species.

TYPES

There are three major types of wetlands:

- Marsh—a wetland dominated by soft-stemmed plants such as grasses, rushes, and sedges.
- Swamp—a wetland dominated by woody plants such as shrubs and trees.
- Bog—a wetland that grows on thick mats of peat, a substance made of partially decayed plants and animals.

All three of these wetland types occur inland and contain fresh water. The terms *marsh* and *swamp*, by themselves, usually refer to these inland wetlands. But they also have coastal versions:

- Salt marsh—a coastal wetland, affected by tides and periodically covered with ocean water, and dominated by soft-stemmed plants such as grasses, rushes, and sedges.
- Mangrove swamp—a coastal wetland, affected by tides and filled with salty ocean water, and dominated by mangrove trees.

PHYSICAL FEATURES

- Wetlands occur on permanently flooded or periodically flooded land.
- They have special soils that develop under waterlogged conditions.
- They are impermanent. Over centuries or thousands of years, wetlands change, developing or disappearing because of many factors, including changes in precipitation, accumulating sediment, and rising sea level.

ANIMALS

- Wetlands have a high diversity of reptilian and amphibian species, from frogs to snakes to crocodiles.
- Long-legged wading birds, many of which have specialized long or large bills, are common.
- Insects have life cycles that include both aquatic and terrestrial forms.
- Large numbers of waterfowl and shorebirds nest in or stop over to feed and rest in wetlands during migration.
- Many endangered species live in wetlands.

PLANTS

- To survive in waterlogged soils, plants have special adaptations such as porous tissues with air spaces to transport air to roots.
- Some plant species in bogs are adapted to catch insects and small aquatic organisms.
- Plants are shallow rooted or may not be rooted in soil at all but float on the water's surface instead.
- Three types of plants inhabit wetlands:
    Emergents—plants, such as grasses and cattails, that grow partly in and partly out of water.
    Floating aquatics—plants, such as water lilies, that float on the water's surface.
    Submergents—plants, such as elodea, that grow entirely underwater.
- Wetlands, except for bogs, are very productive, producing a lot of plant material each year.

⚐ 2 ⚐
NORTH AMERICAN
WETLANDS

From the salt marshes of Mexico's Gulf Coast to the bogs of Canada's tundra, to the moss-draped swamps of the southeastern United States, North America has a wealth of wetlands. And they're crawling with wildlife. In the Everglades, anhingas—diving birds that lack the oil to waterproof their feathers—hold their wings outspread to dry in the sun. Cranes gulp seeds in a wet meadow in Nebraska, while crabs sidestep up a Mexican mangrove tree. In San Francisco Bay, herons gulp down fish, while in a Canadian bog, bears nibble blueberries for lunch. Each region of North America has its own particular mix of wetland habitats. Along with that comes a distinctive animal community.

THE NORTH

Wetlands are widespread in the northern reaches of the continent, where glaciers—mile-thick rivers of ice—sculpted the landscape thousands of years ago. Gouging out holes, scraping the land, and dumping sediment, these glaciers created depressions where wetlands later formed. Today, on these formerly glaciated lands, tundra, taiga, and prairie grow. The Arctic tundra of Alaska and upper Canada is soggy and lumpy with wetlands. The northern coniferous forests, called taiga, are interspersed with damp bogs often ringed by spruce trees.

Farther south, in Manitoba, Alberta, Saskatchewan, the Dakotas, and Minnesota, lies prairie, dotted with prairie pothole marshes. More than half of North America's waterfowl nest on the grassy edges of such marshes. These wetlands range from a fifth of an acre (less than a tenth of a hectare) to 25 acres (10 hectares) in size. They formed where

These farmlands near Manitoba, Canada,
are dotted with prairie potholes.

glaciers left gigantic ice chunks buried in sediment. When these ice blocks melted, the land slumped, forming shallow pits. Later, these depressions filled with rain and snow, creating the wetlands we see today.

Canada, which contains 24 percent of the world's wetlands—314 million acres (126 million hectares)—also has coastal salt marshes along Hudson Bay. Extensive freshwater marshes exist where rivers pour into lakes such as Lake Winnipeg.

THE EAST AND GULF COASTS

Near the East and Gulf Coasts of North America, wide, sluggish rivers make their way to the sea. On bottomlands—low-lying lands where rivers spread out—magnificent, moss-draped cypress swamps grow. Wood ducks, otters, bears, and water moccasins make these swamps their home. In coastal North Carolina, bobcats and bears hide out in pocosins. Pocosins—from the Algonquian word for "swamp on a hill"—are actually bogs clothed with densely packed shrubs and pines.

On the East and Gulf Coasts, the land gently slopes toward the ocean. Bays and barrier islands buffer waves. These conditions allow a fringe of salt marsh to form. Salt marsh runs from southern Massachusetts to Florida and along the Gulf Coast. Ospreys, egrets, muskrats, and mud crabs feed among the waving grasses. Behind these salt marshes are special freshwater marshes filled by river water but affected by the ocean tides. Ocean tides surge through salt marshes and river mouths, which in turn push against the waters of freshwater marshes that lie behind.

THE WEST

In the western United States, wetlands are less widespread. The reason for this is twofold. Inland, the climate is generally dry, so wetlands only form along the narrow margins of

Although wetlands are scarce in the western part of the United States, salt marshes do exist around San Francisco Bay.

rivers and lakes. The coast, for the most part, is steep and wave-prone, so it doesn't support much salt-marsh habitat. However, in certain places such as San Francisco Bay and Washington's Willapa Bay, mudflats and salt marshes do exist. The fact that wetlands are relatively scarce in western North America makes them even more valuable to the people and wildlife of these dry regions.

MEXICO, THE CARIBBEAN, AND FLORIDA'S TIP

Most of Mexico's wetlands, about 6,000 square miles (16,000 square kilometers), lie near its coasts in the form of freshwater lagoons and mangrove swamps. Birds such as brown pelicans, seen in Canadian and United States wetlands, spend their winters in these Mexican coastal lagoons. Manatees, storks, egrets, and pelicans feed in mangrove swamps, which fringe Mexico, the Caribbean islands, and the southern tip of Florida.

WETLAND WONDERLANDS

In the lower forty-eight United States, there are 105 million acres (42 million hectares) of wetland, less than half the amount that existed two centuries ago. Nevertheless, North America still supports an impressive array of wetlands. Here are a few more facts about these remarkable habitats:

- Okefenokee, which means "land of the trembling water," is a wetland region shared by Georgia and Florida. If you step onto its floating islands of plants, you will indeed tremble, or perhaps even sink into the brown waters below. The water is brown because it's stained by decaying leaves that release tannin, the same chemical that makes tea brown.

- Alaska's wetlands are in good condition; very few have been damaged by pollution or development. The state

*The Okefenokee Swamp is
home to a variety of wildlife,
including alligators and egrets.*

contains 170 million acres (69 million hectares) of wetland. That's more than the total wetland acreage found in
all the lower forty-eight United States combined.

- The wetlands on Caribbean islands, although small in
  size, are important to the survival of rare and migrating
  birds. Cuba's Zapata Swamp, the largest of the Caribbean
  wetlands, is a mixture of lagoons, mangrove swamps,
  marshes, and mudflats. It has an endangered crocodile
  plus many endemic bird species—species that live
  nowhere else on earth.

- The Everglades, which stretches from Lake Okeechobee
  south to the tip of Florida, is often called the river of grass.
  A sheet of water 7 inches (17.8 centimeters) deep slowly
  flows through grasslike sedges in a fifty-mile- (eighty-
  kilometer-) wide path.

- In eastern Washington State, 88,000-acre (35,000-hectare) Willapa Bay contains salt marshes and mudflats that provide a feast for tens of thousands of migrating shorebirds and as many as 80,000 nesting waterfowl in a day.

- George Washington was once involved in a project to drain the Great Dismal Swamp in Virginia. Fortunately, the project didn't work out. However, much of the wetland has been drained, ditched, and timbered over the years. The Great Dismal Swamp was once an immense wilderness filled with ancient, wide-trunked bald cypress, Atlantic cedar, and gum trees. Much of that now is gone; but glimpses of its former grandeur remain.

- The marshes of Wood Buffalo National Park, in Canada, are the world's only remaining nesting site for whooping cranes. The endangered birds fly 2,500 miles (4,000 kilometers) from the marshes of Aransas Wildlife Refuge in Texas to those in Wood Buffalo National Park.

A whooping crane on its nest at Wood Buffalo National Park

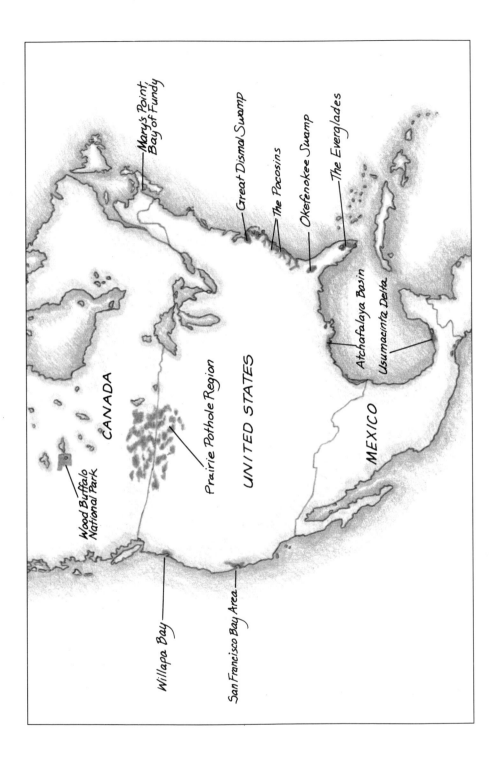

- In the Atchafalaya Basin, one of the largest wetlands in the United States, you can canoe past towering bald cypress trees. You can catch crabs, crayfish, and frogs with a local fisherman and cook up a traditional Creole gumbo—a spicy stew. If you're lucky you might even hear some alligator stories—tales and tails that grow each time they're told.

- Every summer, more than a million sandpipers stop by Mary's Point, the site of mudflats and salt marshes in the Bay of Fundy, New Brunswick, Canada. This is just one of the wetlands where shorebirds feed on a shrimp feast to fatten up for migratory journeys, some of which take them all the way to South America.

- The Usumacinta Delta, a 2.5-million-acre (1-million-hectare) expanse of wetlands, lies on the Gulf Coast of Mexico. The region's mangrove swamps are nursery grounds for shrimp, and home to West Indian manatees—rare, gigantic aquatic mammals. Hundreds of thousands of egrets, storks, spoonbills, and ibis nest here or stop by during their migration.

⚓ 3 ⚓
FRESHWATER MARSHES AND SWAMPS

In spring, a swamp or marsh can be a downright noisy place, so noisy that your ears begin to ring. Spring peepers—frogs so small they fit on a quarter—call "peep, peep, peep" in a piercing tone. Leopard frogs croak "chuck, chuck, chuck!" Chorus frogs belt out their nasal "bree-e-e-e-e." Male frogs call to attract female frogs, who lay eggs the males can fertilize. Marshes and swamps are an excellent habitat for frogs, who spend part of their lives in water and part on land. But these wetlands are also home to herons, snakes, otters, and others who may have tasty tadpoles or frog's-leg dinners in mind.

MARVELOUS MARSHES

Freshwater marshes and swamps form at the edges of lakes and where rivers overflow their banks. They're also found in shallow basins where groundwater seeps or rain and snow collect. Swamps contain woody-stemmed plants such as shrubs and trees, while soft-stemmed plants such as grasses, rushes, and sedges dominate the marsh landscape.

Plant Adaptations Floating water lilies or underwater elodea plants don't need stiff, rigid stems to hold them up. Water supports their leaves. Soft, flexible stems work fine.

Water lilies are a common wetland plant. Flexible stems allow their leaves to float on the water's surface.

Cattails, which grow up into the air, need sturdier stems. Water lilies root in the muddy bottom but have leaves that float on the surface. Extra-long, flexible stems allow their leaves to rise and fall when water levels do.

Wetland plants that root in the wetland mud face the problem of low oxygen. Wetland soils contain very little oxygen; bacteria use it up when decomposing dead material. So, many marsh plants have spongy stems full of spaces. They transport air to their roots through these spaces. Rooting into the mud isn't absolutely necessary, however. Unlike land plants, which absorb minerals and water from the soil, water plants can absorb these necessities from the water all around them instead. Duckweed, for instance, doesn't root into soil. It absorbs minerals through hanging roots and floating leaves.

Pushy Cats   Like hot dogs on sticks, cattails poke up out of marshes. The "hot dog" part is a cluster of tiny flowers—as many as 250,000 on one stem! Once these are fertilized by wind-blown pollen, seeds form, and the cluster of seeds expands. Then it crumbles, and its seeds float away, held aloft by downy fluff. The original cattail clump also spreads by roots. Because cattails spread so easily and can withstand low water levels and pollution, they often crowd out other marsh plants.

The Double Life   Most of the dragonflies living in marshes aren't zipping around in the sky. They're underwater. Dragonflies spend one to five years underwater, as caterpillar-like larvae, before emerging as flying adults. When it's time, they undergo metamorphosis. They crawl up a stem, shed their skin, spread out their wings, and begin their one season as adults. Adult dragonflies are aerial acrobats. They can twist each set of wings independently, and stop, start, hover, and fly at speeds up to 60 miles (97 kilometers) per hour. They even capture insects, mate, and lay eggs, all while on the wing. Many other wetland insects, such as midges, mayflies, and mosquitoes, also live double lives and undergo metamorphosis.

A green darner dragonfly (left) and a damselfly (right) are covered with dew. Note the difference in the position of their wings at rest.

Damselflies, another wetland insect, have a similar appearance and similar life cycle to dragonflies. But you can tell them apart when they're perched. Dragonflies hold their wings out flat, whereas damselflies keep them folded behind.

• COUNTING CROAKERS: THE FROG CHALLENGE •

All around the Great Lakes, in both Canada and the United States, volunteers are out counting frogs. It's all a part of the Great Lakes Marsh Survey, to survey plants, birds, and amphibians. Frog counting can be difficult because hundreds of frogs, of many species, may call at once. So volunteers first learn the calls by listening to tapes.

Out in the field, they record the "call level" of each frog species. For instance, the call level would be 0 if they heard none calling; 1 if they heard some calling but none of the calls overlapped; 2 if some of the calls overlapped; or 3 if there were so many overlapping calls they could hardly distinguish one call from another! When possible, volunteers also estimate the number of frogs in each species. Three surveys are done a month apart, in April, May, and June. Farther north, where spring comes late, they may be done in May, June, and July.

To help do a survey, contact local parks about their junior-naturalist programs, and local Audubon Societies. These groups may have helpful information and news about surveys already in progress. You can also set up your own frog survey, based on the one above. Repeat it each year to build a valuable base of information about the wetland. For tapes of frog calls, check your library or purchase them from: Chelsea Green Publishing Company, Route 113, P.O. Box 130, Post Mills, VT, 05058-0130. Phone 1-800-639-4099.

Bzzzzt! Mosquito Alert! People often blame mosquitoes on wetlands. Sometimes that's unfair, considering that mosquitoes also breed in damp fields, moist forest soils, and even in water-filled discarded tires. But it's true that mosquitoes do breed in tremendous numbers in many wetlands, where there's plenty of water for their aquatic larvae to develop. The winged adults usually feed on nectar. Only the female, just before she lay eggs, needs a blood meal. Mosquito larvae are a major food source for fish, birds, dragonflies, bats, and other wetland residents.

Hidden Wildlife You're more likely to hear a sora's "ker-wee!" or black rail's "kickee-doo" than ever to see these shy, secretive birds. They live in marsh grasses, where their striped, brown bodies blend right in. For extra protection, they dash across open spots to avoid being seen by predators. A close relative, the American bittern, freezes when danger approaches. With its beak pointing up and its striped breast, it looks like a clump of grass. To count these and other elusive birds, scientists rely on sound. They broadcast a tape of the birds' call. The birds, thinking another bird has entered their territory, will usually call back or approach to investigate. Then the scientists can see and count the birds. However, such tapes are only used sparingly, because they can disturb nesting birds.

For the Birds Marshes are home to muskrats, mosquitoes, and rats, and host visiting deer, bobcats, foxes, and raccoons. But in many ways, marshes are the birds' domain. Red-winged blackbirds noisily establish marsh territories in spring. Long-legged waders, such as herons, catch fish by using their S-curved necks to launch their heads forward. Ducks and geese dabble for seeds, roots, and submergent plants, then pause to waterproof their feathers by grooming them with oil from special glands. Fifty to eighty percent of North American ducks breed and raise young in prairie pothole marshes. Many other birds, from warblers to hawks, stop over to feed in marshes during migration.

SWAMP SPECIFICS

In many people's minds, swamps belong to the snakes. People have visions of vipers dropping down from trees to attack them. It's unlikely to happen, at least in North America. Snakes prefer to capture more manageable prey. Wetlands, however, do contain a diversity of snakes, rivaled only by those of the desert. Rattlesnakes, copperheads, and cottonmouths, all of which are poisonous, deserve both caution and a respectful distance. But biting is typically a last-ditch defense for snakes. If you don't bother them, they generally won't bother you. Seeing a snake is rare, and most are not poisonous, so from a distance, enjoy them for the marvel they are. Just look where you're walking or sitting, so neither you nor a snake will be surprised!

Cottonmouths, also called water moccasins, can be found in swamps in the southeastern United States.

Tree-mendous Trees and Diversity   In swamps, where water and minerals are plentiful, trees can grow to impressive sizes. Tree species vary regionally. In Canada's taiga, swamps contain conifers such as spruce, fir, larch, or northern white cedar. In the western United States, flooded forests along rivers contain evergreens such as alder and hemlock. New England swamps are filled with red maple, which turns a vivid scarlet in fall. In the Deep South, from Virginia to Louisiana, swamps flooded year-round are filled with tupelos, water oaks, and bald cypresses—a relative of the redwood tree. The following paragraphs highlight some of the features of swamps with mostly deciduous trees—trees that lose their leaves each fall. These swamps include red maple swamps, southern bottomland hardwood swamps, and cypress swamps of Florida.

Layers of Life   Like rain forests, forested swamps have distinct layers of life: a canopy, a shrub layer, and the flooded forest floor. These wetlands combine some of the species and characteristics of marshes with the complex, layered

---

• SHRUB SWAMP •

Not all swamps are clothed in trees; some have shrubs instead, or a mixture of the two. In the taiga of Canada and Alaska, willow and alder form streamside thickets, a kind of shrubby swamp. The shoots and catkins of willows and alders provide food for grouse, chickadees, snowshoe hares, and even moose. Below their branches, American woodcocks, which are champion worm-eaters, probe the soil with their pencil-like bills. And star-nosed moles, with twenty-two tentacle-like feelers around their snouts, swim and burrow, searching for crayfish and grubs.

---

life of forests. In spring, before trees leaf out, swamp-floor wildflowers can gather lots of sunlight. Smelly skunkweed blooms first. It melts its way through snow and frozen ground with heat it generates itself. Later, green jack-in-the-pulpits, yellow marsh marigolds, white trilliums, and pink liverworts appear. Shrubs such as honeysuckle and azalea bloom later on. Throughout spring and summer, hordes of bees feed and pollinate tree flowers in the canopy, lending a muffled buzzing to the air.

Living on Air   Near Charleston, South Carolina, swamp trees are draped with gray, ghostly Spanish moss. Spanish moss is an epiphyte, meaning it lives on trees. But it doesn't feed off the tree; instead, it just uses it as a perch. Spanish moss lives by absorbing water and minerals from rainfall and dust. It's a bromeliad, a relative of the pineapple. Other bromeliads such as the cow-horn orchid, wild pine, and butterfly orchid inhabit Florida swamps.

Trees With Knees   Bald cypresses have knees—or at least knobs that look like knees. They stick up out of the water near the tree's base. These knobs, which may be up to 12 feet (3.6 meters) high, are believed to help the tree get oxygen, which is scarce in wetland mud. (Scientists aren't sure if this is the function of the knees, but it's the best theory so far.) Another feature of swamp trees is their shallow, widespread roots. Roots close to the surface can get oxygen from the water and the air more easily. But shallow-rooted trees are at risk of toppling. So bald cypress, water tupelo, and gum trees have flared supports called buttresses on their trunks, as rain forest trees do.

Hands Off!   As poison ivy victims know, plants can defend themselves against animals that might eat them,

Spanish moss gives a ghostly beauty to trees in southern swamps.

step on them, or damage their leaves. Swamp-dwelling poison sumac gives a rash worse than poison ivy. Nettles embed themselves in skin and release acid that stings. (Nettles, however, when boiled a few minutes, lose their sting and can be made into soup!) Arrow arum and jack-in-the-pulpit have underground plant parts that are filled with sharp crystals that burn and cut the tongues and mouths of animals that try to eat them.

Good Cavities   Peek in a hole in a tree and you may find a nest. Woodpeckers excavate their nest holes flake by flake. Other birds, such as owls, titmice, wrens, swallows, prothonotary warblers, and chickadees, move into preexisting holes—rotted areas or old woodpecker homes. A dead tree, with its soft wood and many hollows, may be a virtual "apartment house," so it's important that dead trees be left standing and not logged. In recent years, tree cavities have become scarce as trees are cut and swamps are cleared. Many people are putting up specially designed boxes to provide housing for wood ducks, which normally live in swamp-tree cavities.

· A JEWEL OF A PLANT ·

Spotted jewelweed, a plant of inland marshes and swamps east of the Mississippi, is a good plant to know. Its yellow-and-orange flowers provide food for hummingbirds, bees, and ants. (Some bumblebees, which can't enter the plant from the front, sneak in to get nectar by cutting a hole in the flower's side.) Another name for the plant, spotted-touch-me-not, refers to the plant's seed pods, which, when touched, fling their seeds far and wide. Perhaps the best reason to know jewelweed is that it's a Native American remedy for poison ivy. Fresh leaves and stems crushed and applied to the poisoned area seem to help some cases heal. Jewelweed is even used in some commercial remedies sold in stores.

Swamp Soup   With up to 10 tons (9 metric tons) of leaves falling on each acre (two-fifths of a hectare) of swamp per year, swamp waters can become a rich soup of nutrients. Breaking down those leaves into the nutrients that fertilize the soil is a remarkably complex community effort. Worms, insect larvae, and other small creatures chew up leaves. Crayfish shred them. Bacteria and fungi break the scraps down further. The leftovers and droppings of all these creatures contribute to a soup of organic material that small insects and freshwater clams eat. All these organisms, in turn, become food for bigger insects, fish, birds, mammals, and other creatures.

WETLANDS IN FLUX

Just because a marsh is packed with cattails edge to edge doesn't mean it will be that way next year. A booming muskrat population may cut so many cattails that open water returns. A flooding river can bury a marsh in mud. Or sediment and leaves, caught among stems and roots, can fill in the marsh over the years. Eventually, a marsh can become drier upland, where shrubs and trees grow. Swamps, too, can change as time passes. Fires can sweep through, killing off shrubs. Windstorms can blow down trees, creating openings where ferns fill in and light-loving trees thrive. Wetland succession—the replacement of one plant community by another—is not a simple and clear-cut process. Although wetlands can change naturally, often changes in wetlands are caused by people's activities, as we'll explain in chapter 6.

4
BOGS

A bog can be an unsettling place. Wet, cool air chills your skin. Odd, low-growing plants cover the land. The ground looks solid, but moss squishes with each step. If you jump up and down, the ground shakes and rolls and young trees nearby tilt. Even stranger still, some of the plants act like animals, using pits and sticky traps to catch prey.

BOG BASICS

In a forest, fallen leaves, dead plants, and dead animals are decomposed by bacteria, fungi, and other organisms. If these decomposers did not do their job, the dead stuff would just pile up. That's what happens in a bog. Waterlogged with acidic, cold, oxygen-poor water, bogs are an unfavorable habitat for the bacteria that decompose dead material. So very little decay occurs. Year after year, new moss grows on the undecayed moss from the previous year. Plant material piles up, pressing down on plant matter underneath, turning it into dense material called peat. Bogs are wetlands that grow in and on these thick layers of peat.

For Peat's Sake In northern bogs, peat is typically made of sphagnum moss. But sedges and shrub leaves can become peat, too. Peat is so thick and dense that it can be cut into blocks and burned as fuel. It's burned for cooking meals

*Pitcher plants like this one
trap and digest insects.*

and heating houses in some parts of Russia, Scandinavia, Great Britain, and Canada. Large industrial plants burn peat to produce electricity. And peat moss is sold to gardeners, who mix it into soil to improve its consistency.

More Than Peat   In a bog, new moss and sedge grow on top of the peat. Orchids, pitcher plants, cotton grass, leather leaf, Labrador tea, cranberry bushes, blueberry bushes, and evergreen shrubs take root, too. Trees such as spruce, tamarack, pine, and cedar also may grow on a bog, usually at its edges.

Chilly, Acidic, and Nutrient-Poor   Bogs tend to be chillier than the surrounding land because they form in low-lying spots, where dense, cold air sinks in and stays. Any water underneath the bog stays cool because it is insulated by the blanket of peat. Bog waters are nutrient-poor because little decay occurs, so nutrients stay locked up in the peat. And the waters are acidic, because partly decayed moss steeps in the water, making a brown, acidic tea.

Mind-Boggling Variety Bogs vary. Some spread out over the landscape, forming what are called blanket bogs. Others accumulate so much peat that they pile up and up—with peat as much as 40 feet (12 meters) thick. These piles of peat form dome-shaped, raised bogs. Pocosins, a bog type found only in coastal Virginia and the Carolinas, are hills covered by thick shrubby growth of hollies, bays, and pines. Fens, a special kind of bog, get their water from groundwater, which picks up nutrients as it percolates through rock and soil. Fens tend to be less acidic, and have more nutrients than other bogs. So the plants that can grow in them are lusher and more diverse.

Bogs of the World In Canada, bogs are called muskegs. In Europe, they're known as mires, moors, or heaths. But by whatever name, bogs cover 1.5 million square miles (4 million square kilometers) of the earth. Most are found in the Northern Hemisphere—in North America and Eurasia—because glacial action helped form bogs there. Twenty-five percent are in Canada. But bogs do occur elsewhere: in isolated spots on mountaintops; in the Southern Hemisphere—in Chile, Argentina, and New Zealand; and even in the Tropics—in Indonesia, Malaysia, and Brazil.

BOG FORMATION

Bogs tend to form in wet places where decay is slow and plants pile up. These places include springs, slow-moving streams, small lakes or ponds, low ground where water collects, fog-drenched hilltops, and places where groundwater seeps out of hillsides.

From Lake to Bog Lakes and ponds can turn into bogs over hundreds and thousands of years. First, shoreline plants such as sedges become established. Their roots and shoots trap sediment. Other plants such as mosses, wild-flowers, and small shrubs can move in on this muddy sediment. Each year, the leaves of the mosses and other plants die. But they don't decay very quickly. So they pile up, forming a thicker and thicker mat of plant matter, held together by roots. This mat grows like a shelf, out over the pond. It forms a choking collar of plants that may eventually cover the water entirely.

Quake, Rattle, and Roll   Lakes or ponds covered by peat form quaking bogs. Quaking bogs shake and roll if you jump up and down on them. The feeling is something like jumping up and down on a soft waterbed. In fact, what you're standing on is a bed of moss that covers a pond hidden far beneath.

Pocket of the North   By visiting Dolly Sod, a bog in West Virginia, you can get a look at plants that normally live hun-

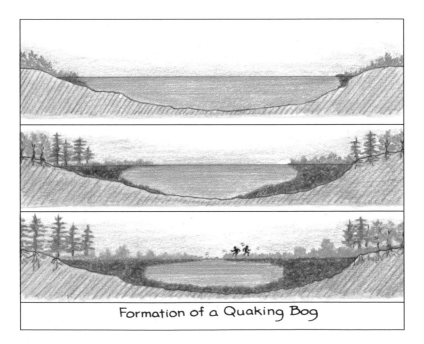

Formation of a Quaking Bog

dreds of miles north. That's because bogs are reservoirs of northern species. During the ice age, these species lived just south of the ice, where conditions were cold. But when the glaciers retreated north, these plants moved north with them. And southern species moved in and took over the land. In bogs, however, cold conditions prevail and many northern species survive to this day.

BOG PLANTS

Like plants in other wetlands, bog plants are adapted to cope with the low oxygen levels in the water. For this reason, many have spongy tissues through which they pump oxygen to their roots. But they also have other unusual adaptations that make them suited for life in bogs.

· THE CASE OF THE BODY IN THE BOG ·

In 1950, several Danish men out cutting peat made a discovery. It was a body, buried 7 feet (2 meters) down in a bog. They thought the body might be from a recent crime. But it turned out, the body was two thousand years old! The man was so perfectly preserved that you could see the expression on his face. His skin was stained dark brown from the bog water. His leather cap was still intact.

Tollund Man, named for the Tollund bog where he was found, is only one of many well-preserved bodies that have been discovered in the peat bogs of northern Europe. The bacteria that usually decompose plants and animals do not thrive in bogs. That's why bodies, and moss, can last for thousands of years. (Bones, however, may dissolve in their acidic waters.) By studying ancient people, woolly mammoths, and even pollen grains trapped in the peat, scientists can learn about animals and plants that lived thousands of years ago.

Water-Conserving Plants With waterlogged roots and a reservoir of water underground, bog plants wouldn't seem to lack for water—but they do! Like tundra plants, bog plants have a hard time absorbing water because the air and soil are so cold. So, they conserve water the best they can. Like desert plants, some bog plants have waxy coverings to prevent water loss. And they protect their stomates—the pores where they exchange gases, where water loss can easily occur. Curved leaf edges, deep pits, or surrounding hair reduces evaporation from these pores. Growing low to the ground helps plants stay snow covered so they'll be insulated from cold and not dried out by wind.

Take a Guess Native Americans used it for their babies' diapers. World War I soldiers used it to bandage wounds. It's acidic, sterile, soft, spongy, and superabsorbent. What's this "miracle" material? Sphagnum moss. Sphagnum moss can hold twenty times its weight in water. Exactly why it's adapted for absorbency, scientists aren't sure.

IT MOSS BE TRUE

Some books say sphagnum moss can absorb 10 times its weight in water. Others say it absorbs 15, 25, 40 times or more. Carry out this experiment and discover the truth for yourself. You'll need:

Sphagnum moss

- Living sphagnum moss (Collect small amounts of the moss from a local wetland, with permission of the owners.)

- A scale (to weigh wet and dry moss)
- Water (to wet the moss)
- A dish (to hold the water)
- A knife or scissors (for cutting moss)
- A pencil and paper (for recording data)

1. Cut three small, living sphagnum moss samples. (A 2-inch- [5-centimeter-] square sample should do.)

2. Shake any excess dirt off the moss.

3. Weigh each sample dry, and record the weights.

4. Squeeze the air out of a moss sample, then submerge it in water and let it expand. Allow it to sit in the dish for a minute to soak up water.

5. Weigh the wet moss sample. Record your results. Repeat steps 4 and 5 with the other samples.

6. Use this formula to determine how much water the moss held:

Wet weight of sample - Dry weight of sample = Weight of water in sample

7. Now compare the amount of water with the dry moss weight, using a different formula:

Weight of water in sample ÷ Dry weight of sample = x

The moss holds x times its weight of water.

Do the calculations for all your samples and average your results.

8. To round out your investigation, examine the moss with a microscope or hand lens. How do you think the moss' structure helps it to hold water?

Coping With Nutrient Scarcity In bogs, because there's very little decay, minerals stay stored in peat. So the minerals plants need for photosynthesis can be scarce. Many plants grow less than they do in areas with more nutrients. In a bog, a tamarack just 3 feet (almost 1 meter) high may be several centuries old. Other bog plants conserve nutrients by being evergreen, meaning they keep their leaves for more than one season. In perhaps the strangest adaptation of all, some plants add insects to their diets. They catch and digest tiny animals in order to get nitrogen, a nutrient they need.

CARNIVOROUS PLANTS

Watch out, flies, fish, and frogs: 450 carnivorous—meat-eating—plants live worldwide. And many of them grow in bogs. Sundews use long, glue-tipped hairs to snag insects that land on their leaves. Venus's flytraps capture flies by snapping their fringed leaves shut, trapping their struggling prey. Other plants use watery pits, smelly lures, and even trigger traps to do the job. Like other plants, carnivorous plants have green stems and leaves. They photosynthesize to make their food. The nutrients these plants gain from digesting prey supplement the nutrients they get from soil.

There are many varieties of sundews. This one is called a roundleaf sundew.

The Tadpole Trap   Scientists once thought the balloonlike bladders on plants called bladderworts were simply air-filled floats. But it turns out these balloons have a different purpose. They're trigger traps, designed to catch swimming prey. When the trap is set, the sides of the bladder are indented. And a tiny door in its wall is shut. Hairs near the door act as triggers. When a tadpole, insect larva, or tiny fish brushes against the hairs, suddenly . . . whoosh! In a fraction of a second, the bladder's door seal is broken and water rushes in, pushing open the door. The prey is carried inside by the rushing water. The door closes and the animal is trapped. It's digested by the plant.

Not a Pretty Pitcher   Pitcher plants have curled leaves that form a pitcher shape. Rainwater falls into the pitchers, forming tiny pools. Special markings and fragrances attract insects to the pitcher's lip. But if they try to land, they slip on downward-pointing hairs. These hairs funnel the insects into the pitcher. If they try to climb out, loose "tiles" stick to their feet, making it difficult to walk. Eventually, the insect lands in the water at the pitcher's base. There, juices digest the insect, and the plant absorbs the nutrients.

Deadly Pitcher-Dwellers   Strangely enough, some animals make pitcher plants their homes. The larvae of mosquitoes, midges, and sarcophagid flies live in the pitcher fluid. (Scientists aren't sure why they don't get digested, along with the other insects.) Spiders build their webs inside the pitcher plant, so they can catch prey that slips and falls in. And frogs sometimes perch on the pitcher lip to catch flies. But that's risky; some fall in and drown! As dangerous as pitcher plants may seem, some are in danger themselves. Many are illegally harvested for floral decorations and are in danger of extinction.

BOG ANIMALS AND THE COMMUNITY

The bog environment is a tough one for animals. There isn't much plant matter to eat. The plants that do grow in bogs are relatively unpalatable. About the only bright spot is the berries. Cranberries, blueberries, and other berries attract bears, sandhill cranes, and people, too. Other conditions make animal life scarce, as well. Bogs' acidic waters are difficult for amphibians and reptiles to withstand. Only a few, such as the endangered Muhlenburg turtle and Pine Barrens tree frog, cope well with the bog environment.

Because of the challenges of bog life, many of the large animals you'll see on bogs are visitors from surrounding land. Deer and caribou feed in bogs. Lynx and fishers—a weasel-like animal—hunt the snowshoe hares, lemmings, and voles that graze there. Beavers cut down trees on forested bogs. And in the evening, great gray owls and short-eared owls can be seen hunting low for mammalian prey.

COASTAL WETLANDS: SALT MARSHES AND MANGROVE SWAMPS

If you travel the coast-hugging roads of Virginia, the Carolinas, and Georgia, you'll see plenty of salt marsh. Snowy egrets feed among waving grasses. Bridges pass over tidal creeks. These salt marshes and their tropical counterparts, mangrove swamps, are bathed in salt water and affected by surging ocean tides. Such conditions are difficult for most plants and animals to withstand. But those creatures that can cope here thrive. Coastal wetlands are home to crabs, crocodiles, cormorants, mosquitoes, manatees, and more.

SALT-MARSH ESSENTIALS

Salt marshes are places of extreme conditions, which change twice daily with the rise and fall of the tides. (Because of geography, a few coasts only have one rise and fall of the tide per twenty-four-hour day.) At high tide, salt marshes are submerged in salty, sometimes cool, ocean water. Yet at low tide, parts of the marsh can be dry and baking in the sun. To cope with these and other salt-marsh conditions, animals have adapted in many unusual ways.

Rise and Fall   As the water level rises, land snails and insects climb up grass stems. As the water level falls, they edge back down. Fiddler crabs, as the time for higher tides approaches, crawl into burrows and plug them tightly with mud. Hours later, at low tide, they emerge and feed. Aquatic animals have the opposite schedule. Low tide is their danger time, when they risk drying out. They hole up in pools and moist burrows when the tide is low. Water snails, however, if caught high and dry, can lose 75 percent of their body water and still survive. When the tide returns, they take up water, swelling to full size within an hour.

Detritus and Other Delights   You'd think the main food in a salt marsh would be the grass. But salt-marsh grass is hard to digest. Only a few organisms, such as marsh crabs, muskrats, grass shrimp, and bacteria, dine on marsh-grass leaves. The main marsh feast is smaller fare: algae, floating organisms called plankton, and detritus. Detritus is a mixture of decaying tidbits of animals and plants and the microorganisms that live on them. Animals gather detritus and algae in several ways. Snails scrape it off grasses. Fiddler crabs sift it from the mud. Mussels filter it from the water all day long. Other salt-marsh dwellers eat bigger foods. Diamondback terrapins—a type of turtle—gulp

Diamondback terrapins can be found along the Gulf and Atlantic Coasts of the United States, as far north as Massachusetts.

down worms. Muskrats eat a variety of foods, as their piles of leftover grass stems, crab claws, and mussel shells reveal.

The Salt-Marsh Café   Salt marshes, especially during fall and spring bird migrations, are a haven for feeding birds. Canada geese, snow geese, dabbling ducks, and American coots eat the seeds of spike grasses and bulrushes. Geese and swans forage for underground stems. Night herons gulp down fish. Long-legged, long-billed birds such as avocets and curlews ply the mud for amphipods, clam worms, and other burrowers. Oystercatchers, with their strong bills,

---

• THE SALT-MARSH SCENE •

Step out of a boat and into an eastern salt marsh. Closest to open water and tidal creeks, you'll find mudflats—exposed areas where algae grow. Fiddler crabs scurry and shorebirds probe the mud for worms. Farther from the water is 8-foot- (2.5-meter-) high salt-marsh cordgrass, its slender leaves dotted with salt. This hardiest of halophytes—"salt-loving" plants—handles salt water by excreting salt through glands in its leaves. Its roots help hold the mud together, permitting the marsh to extend its range.

In the high marsh, where soils are more stable and tides less severe, shorter saltmeadow cordgrass grows in clumps. Purple marsh crabs scurry. Salt-marsh turtles wander, crying salty tears to get rid of excess salt. In places, seawater puddles evaporate, leaving salt pans behind. In these salty circles, only extremely salt-tolerant plants such as glasswort and sea lavender can survive. Farther up the marsh, where the land is rarely flooded, you'll find black grass, salt-marsh pink, swamp rose mallow, pine trees, and bayberry—whose berries perfume soaps and candles.

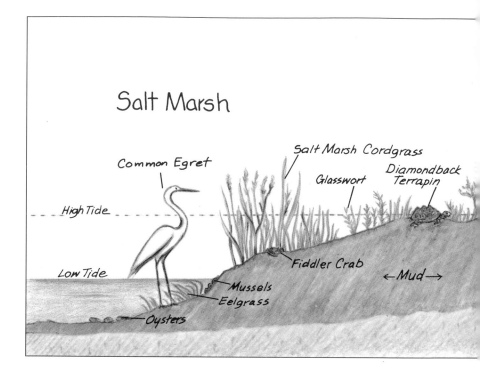

Salt Marsh

Common Egret

Salt Marsh Cordgrass

Glasswort

Diamondback Terrapin

High Tide

Low Tide

Fiddler Crab

←Mud→

Mussels

Eelgrass

Oysters

pry open oysters and eat what's inside. And at dusk, northern harriers and short-eared owls sweep above the marsh, hunting for voles.

Be Productive! Salt marshes are incredibly productive, in terms of how much plant matter they grow each year. They're twice as productive as cornfields, even heavily, artificially fertilized ones. Why are salt marshes so extremely productive? Because they are nutrient-rich. Nutrients are brought in by rivers and ocean tides. And nutrients are supplied by the marsh's own decaying animals and plants. The marsh is constantly bathed in this fertilizing "soup," as nutrients are trapped and recirculated by tides. One acre (two-fifths of a hectare) of salt marsh may produce 4.8 tons (4.3 metric tons) of plants in a year. Salt marshes' productiv-

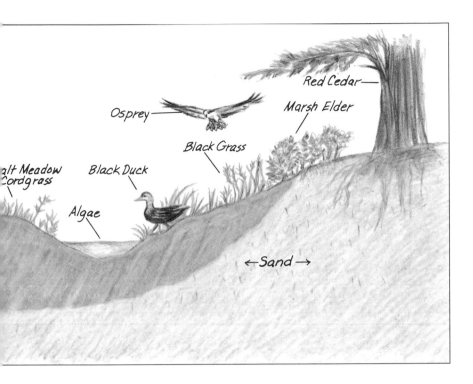

Osprey

Red Cedar

Marsh Elder

Black Grass

Salt Meadow Cordgrass

Black Duck

Algae

←Sand→

ity helps support coastal fisheries and the duck and shore-bird populations of North America.

MANGROVE SWAMPS: THE FRINGING FORESTS

Crabs scurry up shoots, fish swim among roots, egrets preen their feathers, and ibis wade. But you won't find many people strolling through North America's mangrove swamps. It's slow going, stooping under branches, climbing over interlocked roots, and slipping on or sinking into mud. And then, there are the mosquitoes, and alligators . . . and the heat and humidity. (And in Indian mangrove forests, there are the tigers to cope with, too!) Still, an excursion into a mangrove swamp, by canoe, boat, or boardwalk, is worth the trip; nowhere else will you see such an extraordinary tangle of life.

Ibis are just one of the creatures you may see in a mangrove swamp.

Tropical Wetlands   At least 1,000 square miles (2,600 square kilometers) of the southwestern tip of Florida is covered by mangrove swamp. This wetland type fringes the tip of Florida, portions of Louisiana's Gulf Islands, many Caribbean islands, and tropical coasts worldwide. Frost and cold winter temperatures seem to limit the spread of mangroves farther north, where salt marshes grow instead.

March of the Mangroves   Only four of the world's eighty species of mangrove tree live in North and South America.

Florida's mangrove swamps have relatively low-growing trees, often not more than 10 to 20 feet (3 to 6 meters) tall. But in Louisiana, mangrove trees may shoot up to heights of 80 feet (24 meters). Wherever they grow, the four North American mangrove species differ in their requirements. As a result, they colonize the shore in a predictable, regular way. Red mangroves "march out" first, sending roots into shallows and trapping sediment. They create conditions favorable for black mangroves, which fill in behind. Farther back, white mangrove trees grow, and farther inland, another mangrove called buttonwood thrives. Intermingled with buttonwood, on more upland areas, gumbo limbo trees, slash pine, and saw palmetto grow.

Proper Props   On the sandy seashore, regular plant roots wouldn't work well because there isn't stable soil in which to root. So, red mangroves send out prop roots—tough, thick roots that arch down in several directions. They prop the tree up, like a supportive stand. These roots help the trees avoid falling over in storms and hold them steady as the tide comes in and out. Black mangroves, which live farther back from the water's edge, don't have these prop roots because they grow on more stable soils.

Too Much Salt and Other Troubles   Salty water and oxygen-depleted muds are two major challenges for coastal plants. Like salt-marsh grasses, many mangrove species get rid of salt through glands on their leaves. Like plants in many other wetlands, mangroves get oxygen to their roots through special air vessels in their stems. But in addition, red mangroves pull in oxygen from the air through pores named lenticels. Black mangroves send spikelike roots, called pneumatophores, up above the water to gather oxygen.

Traveling Plants To spread to new places and colonize new shores, mangroves float on the sea. Red mangroves produce seeds that sprout and grow into seedlings while they're still attached to the parent plant. Eventually, each seedling will become so heavy, it drops off the plant and floats away. When it bumps into a shoreline—a likely habitat—the young mangrove puts down roots.

Hangers On Sir Walter Raleigh, an English explorer who lived in the late 1500s, believed that mangrove trees made oysters. It's an understandable mistake. Frons oysters are found growing attached to mangrove roots. Many other animal species hang on, too. Anemones with stinging tentacles and jellylike hydroids and tunicates grow attached to mangrove roots. So do snails. Snakes, such as the Florida cottonmouth and the mangrove water snake, twine around mangrove trunks to rest in the sun or shade. Green anoles, a type of lizard, scurry up roots where crabs sidestep their way along. Mangrove swamps are truly a tangle of life with a fascinating community of animals and plants.

Spoons and Storks Long-legged, big-bodied birds are common in mangrove swamps. And each has its own tools and techniques for getting food. Roseate spoonbills swing their sensitive, "spatula"-tipped bills back and forth in the water so they can feel for insects and other prey. Ibis use curved bills for probing the mud and sand. Pelicans, which nest in mangrove swamps, move out to open water to feed. There they dive down and scoop up fish in their 2-gallon- (7.6-liter-) capacity pouches. Up in the mangrove canopy, roseate spoonbills, snowy egrets, green herons, white ibis, and tricolored herons nest. These places are relatively safe from most land-based predators, who won't wade out to them, but snakes and alligators are still a danger. Around

1900, people were the major threat. Egret, heron, and spoonbill populations were almost wiped out by hunters gathering feathers for ladies' hats. Fortunately, this practice was eventually stopped, and the bird populations have slowly recovered.

Cows of the Sea   Marsh rabbits and raccoons may be seen among mangroves. But the big mammal that is most characteristic is the manatee. Manatees, nicknamed "sea cows,"

· MANGROVES AND PEOPLE ·

In Mexico, Central America, South America, and Asia, the wood of mangrove trees is used for cooking food and heating homes. Tannin extracted from the trees is used in curing hides. The sap of one species is even used as an anesthetic for dentistry! But perhaps the greatest value of mangrove swamps is their role as coastal protectors. Mangroves hold the soils of the coast together, buffering shores against storms and preventing erosion. They help protect people, their homes, boats, and boat anchorages. Bangladesh—a low-lying country particularly susceptible to flooding and erosion—has a government-sponsored program to plant more mangroves to stabilize the shore.

Despite their usefulness, mangrove swamps are rapidly being wiped out all over the Tropics. Between 1960 and 1985, one half of Guatemala's mangrove forests were destroyed. The major causes are the clearing of mangroves to create ponds to raise shrimp, and the harvest of mangrove wood for making charcoal used in people's cooking fires. Sprawling urban development causes mangrove forests to be cut for construction material, filled in to provide new land, or polluted by nearby development. Efforts to protect mangrove swamps are only just beginning.

The state of Florida has a number of innovative programs to raise awareness of the manatees' endangered status.

are 13-foot- (4-meter-) long vegetarians that live in the warm waters near mangrove wetlands on Florida's shores. Manatees are *big* eaters, weighing 3,500 pounds (1,600 kilograms) and eating 60 to 80 pounds (27 to 36 kilograms) of aquatic plants a day! These gentle giants are an endangered species. Efforts are being made to protect manatees from the major threat to their existence: power boats. Manatees swim in shallow waters and the propellers of boat motors often cut them when they collide, with tragic consequences.

THANKS TO COASTAL WETLANDS

Next time you eat a fish sandwich or a fried shrimp, thank a salt marsh. Or thank a mangrove swamp. Because these habitats, and nearby waters, are nursery grounds for young fish, shrimp, and crabs. Tides flush detritus out of salt marshes and mangrove swamps into estuaries. There these nutrients form the basis of a food chain. It's a food chain on which fish and shellfish depend.

These fish and shellfish become food for people and for the offshore, big-game fish—tuna, marlin, and swordfish—that people eat. Back in the estuary, clams, mussels, and oysters feed on detritus washed off salt marshes. In places, declining oyster populations have been linked to wetland loss nearby.

Salt marshes and mangrove swamps don't just provide food for people. They're a "filling station" for millions

Western sandpipers feed on a mudflat in Washington State.

of migrating birds. Gulls, terns, plovers, sandpipers, avocets, eagles, and others stop by mudflats to fill up on food before flying on. Mangrove swamps and salt marshes can support many hungry fish, birds, and people because of their tremendous productivity. Nourished by nutrients brought by daily pulsing tides, they manufacture immense amounts of food. These coastal wetland communities form a living fringe critical to both the land and sea.

⚡ 6 ⚡
PEOPLE AND WETLANDS

If you've ever eaten a marshmallow, you have wetlands to thank. The French chefs who invented marshmallows made them gooey by using the roots of marsh mallow, a salt-marsh plant. Aspirin, too, was first made from the willow, a wetland tree. (Native Americans chewed the twigs for pain relief.) Wetlands have always been a treasure trove of edible and medicinal plants, but they offer other benefits, too. Today, many people are recognizing the value of wetland and working to conserve this biome.

THE IMPORTANCE OF WETLANDS
Before grocery stores, pharmacies, and department stores, wetlands were the major place people gathered what they needed. In bogs, you could harvest cranberries. Swamps were the best places for hunting, trapping, and fishing. The first paper was made from papyrus, a wetland plant that grew along the Nile. Reeds, thatches, and palms from wetlands were used to thatch roofs and are still used in Jamaica, the Philippines, and other countries today. In modern times, half the world's people rely on rice, a wetland plant, for most of their food each day. A few other ways wetlands benefit people and the global environment are described on the following pages.

Cranberries are harvested using a thresher to knock the berries off the plant.

Once the threshers have passed through, cranberries float on the surface of the bog.

Held in position by flotation buoys, cranberries are gently pushed toward a conveyor that loads them onto trucks.

EAT A WETLAND (MEAL)

To highlight the importance of wetlands, serve a wetland meal to family and friends. Or, have your class organize a wetland dinner to educate the community and/or raise money for a local wetland project.

MENU

~ Fish ~
Most of the ocean-dwelling fish—mussels, clams, oysters, and shrimp—that we eat depend, directly or indirectly, on the nutrients provided by salt marshes. River and lake fish may also depend on wetland nutrients. You can prepare fish several different ways: fried, baked, or broiled.

~ Wild Rice With Water Chestnuts ~
Wild rice, the seed of a marsh grass, is grown in Minnesota marshes and sold at grocery stores. Three minutes before the rice is done, stir in water chestnuts for an extra crunch. Water chestnuts are the tubers—rootlike, underground parts—of a salt-marsh sedge.

~ Cranberry Muffins ~
Cranberries are native to North American bogs and are grown and harvested commercially in specially maintained cranberry bogs. Make muffins from scratch or use a mix that contains cranberries.

~ Water With Mint ~
Wetlands help purify water by filtering out sediment and toxins before water enters streams, lakes, and underground aquifers. This water provides drinking water, too. For extra taste, add a crushed sprig of mint to the water you serve; mint species are common wetland plants.

Fish Nursery Two-thirds of the fish and shellfish harvested off the Atlantic and Gulf shores of the United States depend on coastal wetlands for their survival. (Half of those caught off the Pacific Coast depend on wetlands, too.) Ocean fish and shellfish spend their larval stages in mangrove swamps, and in estuaries, which get their nutrients from salt marshes. Even freshwater fish often depend on marshes and swamps along rivers and lakes.

Flood Protection When some rivers flood, their floodwaters spread out into the wetlands that border them. There the water is held and slowly released back into the river over a period of weeks and months. Without this kind of storage, dangerous floodwaters are more likely to rush downstream, scouring away riverbed life and destroying bridges, levees, and other structures. Studies have shown that preserving riparian—riverside—wetlands is a cost-effective means of preventing flooding farther downstream. For that reason, some areas flooded during the 1993 Mississippi River floods are being preserved as wetlands for future flood control.

Safeguarding Coasts Blocking high winds and binding soil with their roots, coastal wetland plants help protect bays, estuaries, and shorelines from damaging storms and wave erosion. Mangroves can even grow outward into shallows, helping to stabilize soils and create new land. Because of these benefits, mangroves are being planted in Miami, Florida, to reduce shoreline erosion there.

Water Purification Wetlands help clean water. When water passes through a wetland, it is filtered by wetland plants. And microbes break down contaminants. This produces cleaner water, which runs into rivers and lakes, percolates underground, and may end up in your drinking glass. In wetlands, water may also slow down and sink into soil, recharging underground water supplies.

Wildlife Habitat and Biodiversity Reservoir Wetlands are a critical habitat for wildlife. One-third of North America's endangered and threatened species live in wetlands. Wetlands in general have a high species diversity—a large number of kinds of animals and plants. This diversity of plants is valuable as a genetic resource, for researchers breeding new crop plants. Researchers may also be able to develop new medicines and products from chemicals found in wetland plants and animals. A diversity of species also increases the chance that some of the species will contain the genes that favor survival if conditions change in the future.

Climatic Stabilizer Wetlands help stabilize temperature and humidity in some local areas. That's because water heats up and cools off more slowly than air. For instance, a wetland may remain cool well into summer and cool off surrounding air. Water also evaporates from wetland surfaces, helping form clouds and rain. And wetlands play a role in the global balance of elements such as oxygen, nitrogen, and carbon. Scientists are only beginning to under-

Canoeists paddle through a patch of water hyacinths in Louisiana's Atchafalaya Basin.

• THE AMAZING WATER-CLEANING WETLAND •

When residents of Arcata, California, faced the problem of upgrading their sewage system, they found a unique solution: build a wetland. Now Arcata has a sewage-treatment center, wetlands, and a city park, all rolled into one.

Dirty water from people's sinks, bathtubs, toilets, and other sources runs into the city's treatment plant. There it is partially treated in settling tanks and oxidation ponds. Afterward, the water is pumped through a string of marshes for further cleaning. Marsh plants filter out many impurities. Wetland microbes break down some of the pollutants. The water emerges, cleaner and clearer, and flows into a nearby river.

By building the marshes, Arcata residents avoided paying for a new, expensive treatment plant. Their marsh solution costs slightly less than other sewage treatment plants, which use expensive machinery. The marshes are also a magnet for bird-watchers, who have found at least two hundred bird species there. People stroll or jog on paths bordering the marshes. And despite the mucky job the marshes do, they don't smell like sewage at all.

Using wetland plants to filter pollutants is being tried in many other locales, from San Diego to Calcutta to Disney World. So far, it seems to work best for sewage from houses and small businesses. In places where industrial plants pump a lot of waste into sewage systems, industrial toxins may kill off marsh plants.

stand wetlands' complex relationship to the balance of these elements in the global climate.

Recreation, and More   Birdwatchers, hikers, hunters, fishermen, photographers, canoe paddlers, and others benefit from wetlands and the streams, lakes, and estuaries nurtured by wetlands. Tourist industries based on wetlands, such as those in Louisiana's bayou country, bring millions of dollars to local communities. Other wetland values are harder to measure in dollars and cents, yet are important nonetheless. Wetlands serve as places of solitude and wilderness in an increasingly crowded world. For many people, nothing matches the feeling of canoeing through a marsh, where the only traffic noise comes from ducks, splashing down.

THREATS TO WETLANDS

Each year, 300,000 acres (120,000 hectares) of wetland are destroyed in the United States. The chief cause of wetland destruction is conversion to farmland. Wetland soils, when farmed, provide rich agricultural yields. But their destruction has been disastrous for water quality and wildlife. In California's Central Valley—where most wetlands have been converted to farmland—the visiting population of waterfowl has decreased by 84 percent since 1940. Since the 1960s, one-half of the prairie potholes in North Dakota have been drained, filled, or farmed. During that same period, North America's waterfowl, which nest and feed in such marshes, have drastically declined.

Development and Pollution These days, filling and draining wetlands for development—homes, malls, airports, and so on—is a major cause of wetland loss. And those wetlands that aren't drained or filled are often harmed by pollution from development nearby. Rainwater washes pesticides, fertilizers, gas, oil, and other pollutants off farm fields, lawns, and parking lots, and into wetlands. Pollution from mines, industrial plants, power plants, and leaking underground storage tanks contaminate wetlands as well.

· WETLAND POLITICS: A REAL QUAGMIRE ·

Over the last twenty years, significant wetland laws, part of the Clean Water Act, have existed in the United States. Yet wetland loss has continued at a rapid rate. Part of the trouble, environmentalists say, is that the law is not being enforced properly. Only a tiny fraction of the people who break the law are prosecuted. Also, many people drain and fill wetlands, then apply for and receive "after the fact" permits, which forgive them for breaking the law. So there's little incentive to follow the law in the first place.

At the same time, many small landowners believe that wetland regulations are too restrictive and unfairly limit what they can do with their property. Building a house, a barn, or a pond on their wetland property can mean filling out a lot of paperwork. And such a building permit may be denied. Even some environmentalists have agreed that regulations need to be improved to address the concerns of small landowners. But they are alarmed by the ways a few people are proposing that the problem be solved.

Dams, Diversions, and Water Scarcity Sometimes federal and state governments carry out gigantic construction projects to change the flow of rivers and streams. They dam rivers to provide electricity, build concrete channels and levees to control flooding, and divert water through pipes to irrigate fields. These projects destroy wetlands by flooding them, draining them, or cutting off their water supplies. Such projects destroyed the wetlands in California's Central Valley. The James Bay Hydroelectric Project in Canada will drown many bogs. The Mississippi River's wetlands, in

Some private landowners and large real estate developers feel wetland regulations unfairly take away from the value of their property. As a result, in 1995 Congress passed legislation that severely limits wetland regulations on private property. For real estate developers, this is good news. Wetland property can be extremely valuable land. Sites for expensive lakefront, ocean-front, and riverfront houses and condominiums are often on freshwater marshes, saltwater marshes, and mangrove swamps. And people are flocking to coastal areas, so pressure to build is intense.

But what about the value of the wetlands to the rest of the community? The benefits of wetlands cleaner water, coastal protection, flood control, wildlife habitat, and so on, are spread out over the whole community. If wetlands are destroyed, the community may have to pay for these services or bear the health risks and economic risks of their loss. All these issues are part of the wetland debate and make choices concerning wetlands and private property rights more difficult.

Louisiana, are starved for sediment, once brought by floods, that is now held upstream by locks and dams.

Sea-Level Rise Some, but not all, scientists predict a global rise in sea level in the next century because of global warming caused by air pollution. If the sea level rises, many low-lying coastal wetlands will be flooded and destroyed. Normally, a rising sea level, which has happened naturally in the past, would simply shift the wetlands farther inland. But today, these areas are mostly covered by buildings, pavement, roads, and so on; therefore such shifting is unlikely to occur.

More Reason for Concern Threats to wetlands vary from place to place. In Canada and northern Europe, peat moss is being mined, causing wholesale destruction of bogs. In the southeastern United States, endangered pitcher plants are illegally harvested, stolen from national parks. In Florida, water hyacinth, a fast-growing, nonnative plant, is clogging waterways and displacing native wetland plants. These problems, plus other threats to wetlands, combine to create a serious environmental problem indeed. As a result, wetlands today are the focus of lawsuits, legislation, conferences, concern, and debate.

CASE STUDY: THE EVERGLADES

Florida's Everglades is the largest freshwater marsh in the United States and one of the world's biological treasures.

Airboats are sometimes used to get around in the Everglades.

· WETLAND CREATION AND RESTORATION: ·
SCIENCE OR FAKERY?

Take some land, add water and plants, and you have a wetland. At least that's what some people would have you believe. Recently, in an attempt to stop the loss of wetlands, government regulators have allowed people to destroy one wetland if they create a comparable wetland elsewhere. But is an artificial wetland a suitable replacement for a fully developed marsh full of wildlife, or a swamp filled with century-old trees? The question remains. Wetland restoration—the science of creating and restoring wetlands—is still in its infancy. Although progress is being made in developing functioning wetlands, much more needs to be learned. Yet as human population grows and consumer demand for development increases, wetlands are increasingly more likely to be destroyed to satisfy those demands.

It's home to alligators, storks, turtles, kites, snakes, and butterflies. But it's also a habitat in trouble. Half of the Everglades has been drained and converted for farmland and other development. In the remaining wetland, breeding populations of wading birds have decreased by 90 percent. Thirty-three of its animal species are endangered. Much of the slow-moving, nourishing sheet of water that once flowed through the Everglades has been diverted for growing sugarcane.

Changes on Tap   Beginning in the early 1900s, federal and state water-control projects drastically changed the flow of water in south Florida. The intent was to drain land for farmland, control flooding, irrigate fields, and provide drinking water for a growing population. Today 1,900 miles (3,000 kilometers) of canals and levees channel the water. Water goes first for drinking-water needs and second to agriculture. What's left, which may be a small amount and can be very polluted from nearby agriculture, is channeled to the Everglades. Most of the time the Everglades receives too little water. (Although at times it may receive too much.) Low water levels have caused a decline in species such as the apple snail and the Everglades snail kite, which dines solely on apple snails. Aggravating already critical problems, cattails, which are pollution-tolerant, are pushing out saw grass and other native plants.

Today, state government, national government, and local people are working together to save the Everglades. Millions of dollars are being spent to restore the habitat. The Army Corps of Engineers, the same agency that built the canals and levees, is now taking a few apart, and they are redirecting water to the Everglades. Much work is left to be done to restore the Everglades. But some important first steps have been made toward saving this magnificent wetland region.

THE FUTURE OF WETLANDS

Many wetland benefits may go unnoticed until wetlands are destroyed and the benefits disappear. But the expense of artificially controlling floods, purifying water, and carrying out other wetland "services" is quickly adding up for some communities. Many more people are beginning to recognize both the usefulness and the beauty of wetlands. Below is a sampling of wetland-saving efforts they're carrying out worldwide:

• All around the Great Lakes, volunteers are identifying plants, and counting birds and frogs. It's all a part of the

Serious conservation efforts are essential now
if wetlands are to be preserved for the future.

Great Lakes Marsh Survey, to study the changes in these important wetlands over several years.

- Canada, the United States, and Mexico have banded together to create the North American Waterfowl Management Plan, which will help conserve the wetlands on which so many waterfowl depend during migration and nesting. The program involves buying and protecting some land and encouraging landowners to protect the rest.

- In California's Central Valley, some farmers are making their farm fields into part-time wetlands to benefit birds. They flood farm fields after the corn harvest so that migrating ducks and geese can rest and feed in these areas during fall and winter. In spring, the fields are dried out and replanted with corn.
- In El Salvador, villagers periodically patrol El Jocotal Lagoon to protect it against wildlife poachers and ranchers who would drain it for grazing land. From the wetland, local people harvest fish, shrimp, and duck eggs. By putting up nesting boxes, they've helped increase duck populations.

With all these people working to help conserve swamps, bogs, and marshes, these wetlands have a fighting chance. But preserving wetlands will require an ongoing commitment to dealing with the challenges they face. Help is needed on many fronts—from writing letters, to planting saw grasses, to studying birds. To find out how you can get involved in conserving wetlands, read the next section.

RESOURCES AND WHAT
YOU CAN DO TO HELP

Here's what you can do to help ensure that wetlands are conserved:

• Learn more by reading books and watching videos and television programs about wetlands. Check your local library, bookstore, and video store for resources. Here are just a few of the books available for further reading:

America's Wetlands by Frank Staub (Carolrhoda, 1995).
The Audubon Society Nature Guide to Wetlands by William A. Niering (Knopf, 1985).
The Field Guide to Wildlife Habitats (volumes on the Eastern United States and Western United States) by Janine M. Benyus (Simon and Schuster, 1989).
Northwoods Wildlife, A Watcher's Guide to Habitats by Janine M. Benyus (NorthWord Press, 1989).
"Our Disappearing Wetlands," by John Mitchell, *National Geographic* (October 1992).
The Vanishing Wetlands by Trent Duffy (Franklin Watts, 1994).
Walking the Wetlands, A Hiker's Guide to Common Plants and Animals of Marshes, Bogs, and Swamps by Janet Lyons and Sandra Jordan (John Wiley, 1989).
Wetlands by Max Finlayson and Michael Moser (Facts on File, 1991).

Wetlands in Danger, A World Conservation Atlas edited by Patrick Dugan (Oxford University Press, 1993).

• For more information on conservation issues related to wetlands, contact your state or province natural resource department, fish and game department, local Audubon chapter, museums, nature centers, and wildlife refuges. You could also contact the following organizations:

Chesapeake Bay Foundation
162 Prince George Street
Annapolis, MD 21401-9983
Phone 1-410-268-8816

United States Fish and Wildlife Service
Publications Unit
4040 North Fairfax Drive
Suite 130
Arlington, VA 22203
Phone 1-703-358-1711

• To find out where wetlands are or were located in your area, contact the United States Geological Survey for a National Wetlands Inventory map of your county. You can call them at:

U.S. Geological Survey
Phone 1-800-USA-MAPS.

• Get your class, ecology club, 4-H Club, Girl Scout troop, Boy Scout troop, or other organization involved in monitoring and preventing pollution in a wetland near you. Have your teacher, leader, or adviser contact one of the following organizations for information:

Global Rivers Environmental Education Network (GREEN)
721 East Huron
Ann Arbor, MI 48104
Phone 1-313-761-8142
Internet: green@green.org

(They teach water monitoring and also sponsor computer conferences linking teachers, students, and citizens working on river, lake, and wetland issues worldwide.)

National Project Wet
Culbertson Hall
Montana State University
Bozeman, MT 59717
Phone 1-406-994-5392

(This organization publishes a variety of water-related educational guides and can connect educators with Project Wet activities and coordinators in their state.)

- Call your local park about wetland activities. Often park naturalists put on special programs called "swamp stomps" where you can really experience wetlands by wading in! Don't try swamp stomping on your own, however. You could hurt yourself and the wetland, too.

- Survey a nearby wetland and keep a record of the plant and animal species you find there. You may want to contact a naturalist for help. Repeat your survey each year, to build a valuable base of information about the wetland. Share what you've found with others. It's best to learn the animals' sounds, because often they can be hard to see. So memorize the animals' calls. For tapes of frog and bird calls, check your library or purchase them from:

Chelsea Green Publishing Company
Route 113
P.O. Box 130
Post Mills, VT 05058-0130
Phone 1-800-639-4099

• Turn off lights, televisions, and other appliances when you are not using them. Saving electricity can prevent the need for coal mining, peat mining, and hydroelectric dams, all of which damage wetlands. Encourage your family to use energy-saving devices in your home. For more energy-saving tips, contact your local electric utility. For a catalog of energy-saving appliances and other environmental products, write to:

Real Goods
966 Mazzoni Street
Ukiah, CA 95482-3471
Phone 1-800-762-7325

Seventh Generation
Colchester, VT 05446-1672
Phone 1-800-456-1177

• Find out where your water comes from. Then work to reduce your water use. The less water you use, the more water is available for aquatic animals and plants. Try taking shorter, more efficient showers and use less water when you brush your teeth. Your family might be able to install more efficient showerheads, faucets, and low-flow toilets. Reduce the amount of water used on lawns by watering in the evening when less water evaporates. Better yet, replace lawns with other kinds of plants that are native to your area and don't require as much water. For information on water-saving devices, see the catalogs above.

- Reduce your use of toxic household substances that can eventually end up in wetlands. For alternatives to commercially produced toxic products, see the catalogs above. For a catalog of less toxic household paints, wood finishes, and leather polishes, contact:

Livos Plant Chemistry
2641 Cerrilos Road
Santa Fe, NM 87501
Phone 1-505-988-9111

- Educate others about wetlands. Put on a skit at school or construct a display for the hallway or a local mall to raise awareness of wetland issues.

- Write letters to state and national government officials telling them how you feel about wetland conservation.

GLOSSARY

biome an area that has a certain kind of community of plants and animals. In the case of terrestrial biomes, but not in aquatic biomes, they have a certain climate as well.

bog a wetland covered with a layer of peat

bromeliad members of the plant family Bromeliaciae; many of these plants are epiphytes

cypress knees the parts of a cypress tree that stick up from the roots and look like knobby knees

detritus pieces of waste material—dead plants, dead animals, animal droppings, and so on—and the microorganisms that live on this material

epiphyte a plant that grows on another plant but does not get its nutrients from that plant

erosion the wearing away of particles of rock or soil by wind, water, and other forces

hydrologic cycle the global circulation of water through lakes, streams, rivers, groundwater, the ocean, and the atmosphere

mangrove swamp   a coastal wetland where mangrove trees grow

marsh   a wetland dominated by grasses

metamorphosis   a major change in the structure of an animal's body as it develops from a larva into an adult

mudflat   a broad, level area of mud often found near marshes

nutrient   a chemical needed by a plant for photosynthesis or by an animal for growth and survival

peat   a dense, often compressed, layer of undecayed or partially decayed plants such as moss

plankton   a small, even microscopic, plant or animal that floats in the water

pocosin   a special bog type that forms a hill with shrubs growing over it

prairie pothole   a small wetland formed by glaciers and found in North America's central grasslands—the prairies

props   specialized mangrove roots that grow down diagonally and help stabilize the tree so it won't fall over

quaking bog   a bog that has water deep underneath its peat layer and therefore shakes when a person steps on it

salt marsh   a coastal wetland periodically flooded with salt water and dominated by grasses and grasslike plants

sediment   particles of material that are transported and deposited by water, wind, or ice

shrub swamp   a wetland dominated by small, woody plants: shrubs

succession   the replacement of one ecological community by another as environmental conditions change

swamp   a wetland dominated by trees

tide   the periodic rise and fall of ocean levels

wetland   land that is periodically flooded

INDEX

PHOTO CREDITS